Do Come In

Do Come In

and Other Lizzie Borden Poems

by Larry W. Allen

PearTree Press

Fall River, Massachusetts

Some of these poems first appeared in *The Hatchet: Lizzie Borden's Journal of Murder, Mystery & Victorian History.*

Poems from *The Hatchet* are reprinted by permission of PearTree Press, © 2007, 2008 by Larry W. Allen.

PearTree Press
P.O. Box 9585
Fall River, MA 02720

© 2008 PearTree Press
Text © 2008 by Larry W. Allen

LIBRARY OF CONGRESS CONTROL NUMBER: 2008936791

ISBN-13: 978-0-9819043-0-6   ISBN-10: 0-9819043-0-0

Cover design: Lizzie Borden by Rick Geary © 2008, All Rights Reserved.
Illustrations: Stefani Koorey

For our grandchildren,
and the history they will know.

Contents

LIST OF ILLUSTRATIONS

Introduction

We all know the ditty:

Lizzie Borden took an axe,
Gave her mother 40 whacks.
When she saw what she had done,
She gave her father 41.

Those who study the case, or read a bit beyond the regular Internet fare, know that this little poem is remarkably incorrect on almost *every* point—the murder weapon was not an axe, but a hatchet; the woman murdered was not Lizzie's mother, but her stepmother; Abby Borden was dealt 19 blows, not 40; and Andrew Borden's body had 10 wounds, not 41. Oh, and let us not forget the *biggest* mistake: Lizzie Borden was acquitted of these crimes, so to assert that she was the perpetrator is not in keeping with the ruling of the court.

Poor Lizzie. To be remembered by generations of jump-ropers as a monster of such proportions seems a crime in and of itself. Nonetheless, this is her history—and our folklore.

Even so, we must remember that this is a *poem*. And poems are allowed artistic and factual license. Poems are not meant to be narratives of truth, but expressions of the inner thoughts and feelings of the poet and/or the subject. Beauty, intensity, style, and rhythm are regarded as characteristics of the poetic form.

This factually inaccurate ditty about Lizzie Borden perfectly captures the essence of what makes this story continue to reverberate into the 21st century. It is a sublime detailing of a horrific crime that shocked the nation and the city of Fall River, Massachusetts, in its waning industrial heyday. Today, those who do not know exactly who Lizzie Borden was, remember this poem and can finish the refrain once they hear the first line. This simple four-line poem has become part of the ether.

And this says a lot about why anything written about Lizzie Borden still resonates, enthralls, and captures our imagination. Fairly or not, she has become a nightmare creation, a Halloween costume, a cautionary tale. She has been converted from a real person to a construct. Like it or not, Lizzie Borden is in the water supply.

Stefani Koorey, Ph.D.
Editor/Publisher of *The Hatchet*

Do Come In

Lizzie

Immortalized in song,
Right or wrong,
You defied your parents
In the strongest way.

Sister Emma,
Quieter and kinder,
Warned against
Such impudence.

Maggie the maid,
Standing by silently,
Spotted the bloodied dress
You had to burn.

Lizzie, even Midol
Could not stop
Your mad cycle
Through an unloving family.

Finding Herself

. . .

Crane's Caskets

Like lettuce in a refrigerator crisper,
loved ones nestle in a Crane's Patented Casket.
Guaranteed or your money back!
And each one comes with a glass viewing window,
so you can dig them up periodically to have a peek!

They come in a variety of sizes, too!
Remember, if Mom won't fit, we must remit!
(And don't worry, we'll MAKE her fit!)
Buy the finest! Crane's Patented Caskets!
Available exclusively through
Almy and Borden, your Fall River area dealers!

No Beau For Lizzie

There will be no beau for Lizzie.
No fancy house,
no suitable clothes,
no social status.

There will be no Rock Street Romeo,
no Highland hero to call
on that industrial street
with its liveries and bakeries and bars.

No longer a nymph at thirty-two,
there will be no beau for Lizzie.

The Grand Tour

Maybe the Tower Of London
with its dank halls and locked rooms
reminded her of home.

The tour of royal heads
and chopping block positions
may have served as inspiration.

Perhaps the fine gowns on display
and shining armor with no knights
told her what she did not have.

Maybe it took Scotland's Wallace Tower,
erect on the hill at Sterling,
to spur her to action.

Time to get home, Lizzie,
and make some changes.

Killing Pigeons

A killer with an axe
lurks in the loft
of the Borden barn.

It is Andrew,
killing Lizzie's pigeons
to stop the neighbor boys
from stealing them.

This perverse logic only works
when you realize
property is money,
and money is what Andrew Borden
is all about.

The mad flutter of wings
cannot drown out Lizzie's cries.
It is not the first time
she has been violated by her father.
Her leviathan outrage
will one day fuel her actions.

Meanwhile she moves in
to clean up his mess,
to gather and bury bodies and heads,
and clean the axe.

A Word From Our Sponsor

Try Mandy Miller's Mutton Broth,
the older it gets the better it gets!
Wonderful with overripe bananas!
And Mandy Miller's Mutton Broth
needs no refrigeration.
Use it as a bug repellent,
the flies won't even want to come in!
Save bowls of Mandy Miller's Mutton Broth
to glue on peeling wallpaper,
It's great for scrapbooking too!
Mandy Miller's Mutton Broth,
available at your favorite store.
Try some today!

The House With No Halls

It is summer
In the house with no halls,
With no way to avoid the heat,
Or the sight of her stepmother,
Or the sound of her inheritance
Slipping away.

Perhaps Emma is right.

The Deed Is Done

. . .

August 4th, 1892

Huge, pale eyes glow
in the semi-gloom
of that shuttered room.

Now the fiend flies toward her
and flings a glancing blow.
She falls to the floor
and the fiend mounts her
like a great cat
raining blow after blow
again and again,
savage and relentless.

Later it is father's turn
as he lounges on the couch.
The lunatic lunges with
blows delivered through tears.

It is a grim business
fueled by a strange mixture
of reluctance and determination,
leviathan outrage . . .
and love.

The Crowe Hatchet

It arches through the air
on its own space odyssey.
Barely missing the
branch of a pear tree,
it executes a half twist
and lands with a soft thud
on the roof of John Crowe's barn.

Newly washed,
it glints in the summer sun,
and points,
like an accusatory magnet,
back to the Borden house.

Maggie the maid
is napping
in her attic room.
The city hall bell
chimes eleven times,
and as if on cue . . .
Lizzie calls.

Do Come In

Someone has served mutton broth
and overripe bananas, again.
Someone has tried to buy prussic acid.
Someone has a blue dress to burn.
Someone has levitated in the barn loft
leaving no footprints in a search for sinkers.
Someone has eaten entirely too many pears.
Someone has hidden a hatchet in the chamber pot,
or down in the cellar covered with ash.
Someone has abused her stepmother in a most unseemly way.
Someone has worn a coat inside out,
or stood naked before him
with a flash of flesh and blade.

Oh, do come in,
someone has killed father.

Crime Scene Photographs

The grainy pictures haunt us.
We want to look and
we want to look away.
The bottoms of Abby's shoes
we find somehow disturbing,
not to mention the darkness on the floor.

And father looks so peaceful
if not a bit uncomfortable on the couch.
We cannot make out a face
because there is no face.

We long for another photograph
of Abby and Andrew together again
side by side,
sort of an American Gothic
from New England.

Under The Village Elms

Under the village elms
Andrew Borden lies dead on the sofa.
Blood splatters the picture,
The walls, and the floor.

His pose is rather
Half on and half off
Of the sofa.
He lies on his side,
Feet still on the floor.

Couples still walk
The village green.
The trees bear the full bloom
Of spring.

The Bug-Eyed Man

Doctor Handy saw him
frantically fleeing
that horror house on Second Street.

He was that famous
bug-eyed man;
that original boogie,
slobbering and crying,
red-faced and running
for all he was worth.

Like the second coming
of Jack The Ripper
on vacation
in New England.

John Morse

He is Lizzie's uncle,
an infrequent visitor
to the Borden home.
He arrived yesterday without baggage
and spent the night in the guest room.

He will be there again tonight
despite the blood on the walls and floor.

Uncle Morse has spent the day downtown
establishing an alibi,
memorizing the names of street car conductors,
introducing himself to strangers,
like he is running for office.

Now he is back
hanging around the yard
eating pears.
Oblivious to the throng of onlookers.
Oblivious to the gaggle of police officers
coming and going.

He takes his time eating those pears.
It's like he doesn't want to go inside,
It's like he already knows.

Secret Of The Cellar

Two pair of eyes,
at nearly nine at night,
wind through the rooms
in the house with no halls.

Alice Russell holds the lamp
and Lizzie the chamber pot
past the bloody couch.
The nude bodies of
Andrew and Abby
lie on the dinning room table,
covered with sheets.

The girls are going
to the privy in the cellar.
They creep through the house
like figures in a Dutch painting.
Alice is trembling,
Lizzie is like stone.
Police outside, watch through the window.

Their business complete,
the ladies return to Lizzie's room.
But fifteen minutes later
Lizzie makes the trip again,
alone this time.
The lamp lighting her way
to another corner of the cellar.
She stoops in front of the sink
beside a pile of bloody clothes.
Hiding a hatchet?
Or adding bloody clothes to bloody clothes?
Nobody knows.

Burning A Bedford Cord Dress

It is light blue with navy diamond figures.
Stained and badly faded, she says,
maybe three months old.
The police had searched for days
and never found it.

There in the kitchen,
in broad daylight,
Three days after the murders,
a drama unfolds.

Why don't you burn that old dress? asks Emma.
So with a wicked smile,
Lizzie suddenly pulls the dress
from a narrow coal closet
and unfurls it like a flag.

With a pinch of prim and proper
and a dash of daring-do,
she tears the dress into strips,
and feeds them individually
to the flames.

Alice Russell is mortified.

A navy blue Bengaline Silk dress
is later shown to the jury.
It is spotless . . . naturally.

Alice Russell's Lament

Please, please
I don't want to hear
that the milk was tainted,
that the bread was poisoned.
I don't want to hear
that someone might do something,
that you were in the barn
looking for iron to mend a screen,
and then hear you change your story.

Please, please
I don't want to see
you change your dress in Emma's room,
or see that bundle on her closet floor.
I don't want to see
you burn that Bedford cord,
and then wonder why no one stopped you.

Please, please
I don't want to hear or see these things.
Someone might have to do something.

Another Word From Our Sponsor

For really sharp tools
depend on Underhill Edged Tools.
Axes and hatchets are our specialty.
Super sharp . . . super dependable.
Whether for business or pleasure
careful craftsmen say Underhill
is a name you can trust!
And our wonderful new shingling hatchet
is only forty eight cents.
It comes fully polished with a gilt edge
and a sturdy hickory handle.
So surprise your family
and astonish your friends
with a sharp tool from Underhill!

The Ordeal

. . .

Lizzie On Trial

She is every bit the lady,
queenly in her black dress
and plumed hat,
black gloves, and long black fan.
Head held high,
she weeps and faints
at appropriate intervals.

She is every bit the devil.
Bolts of lightning fly from her eyes.
She wears an evil grin
and her hair is filled with snakes.
One can only look at her
obliquely . . .
or face a fear of stone.

Don't Worry Little Girl

Everything
will be alright.
Soon you will be free.

Free to buy new clothes
and that house
on the hill.

Free to have servants,
to shop in Boston
and New York.

Free to have gay parties
and enjoy your wildlife friends.
To live your life alone and free.

Free and alone, little girl,
everything will be alright.

Cordiality

It depends on one's idea
of cordiality.

Good morning, Mrs. Borden!
Delicious mutton broth!
Lovely dress, Mrs. Borden!
Are you going out?
Have a nice day, Mrs. Borden!

Be courteous.
Always say good morning.
Curtsey often.

Chop, dice, repeat.
Chop, dice, repeat.

As Fall River Turns

Eli Bence
waits in the drug store
for Lizzie.

He has read the script.
After today he will be a star.
Today he will refuse to sell
prussic acid to Lizzie Borden.

Soon he will be called
to testify
at the inquest and the trial.
He will have the goods
on Lizzie Borden.

He will go on tour
and tell his story
like Bob and Charley Ford,
pointing out where each person stood
and what they said.

He will get bigger and bigger parts.
He will be a star,
if no changes are made,
if they follow the script.

Try It Yourself

Try it yourself.
Use a rolled up newspaper
or a magazine
or even this book,
and strike the table
nineteen times . . . HARD.

Imagine the anger,
the wild eyed
drooling hatred,
the pee-in-your-pants
ferocity
of blade biting bone.

Hard to imagine
the insanity
unless you
try it yourself.

Probably Guilty

You are probably guilty,
Said the Judge.
Probably guilty
Of shoplifting,
Of homosexuality,
Of incest,
Of murder.

Probably guilty.

You will be judged
By a jury of your peers,
With no women allowed, of course,
But you are probably guilty.

Even if acquitted
You will be judged
By the community
And found guilty again.

Probably.

Andrew Borden's Skull

If Andrew Borden's skull could talk
with unhinged jaw wobbling back and forth.
If we could fashion a voice box
with plywood and bailing wire
and force air past those lipless teeth.
If sightless sockets could somehow see
or earless ears could hear
a whispered word like "father."

If Andrew Borden's skull could talk.

The Purple Vial
with apologies to William Carlos Williams

so much depends
upon

a purple vial of prussic
acid

on an apothecary
shelf

beside the white
lozenges.

Me And Brownie

It was playtime for me and Brownie, you see.
We was playing.
And when they wouldn't let us in the house,
me and Brownie,
We went to the barn.
We was after the killer, see?
Me and Brownie,
we played around,
kicking at the straw and stuff.
We messed around in the loft too, see?
But after a while we left,
Me and Brownie.
We didn't see nothing.

Twelve Good Men And True

They sit like gnomes
with beards in their laps.
Twelve good men and true
who look upon her as their
Snow White, to care for and protect.
As their frail and virtuous daughter,
sister, wife and lover.
They see no blood, no weapon
or reason she is here.
Now they must file out
with minds made up
and a hour to kill.

What Say You?

Lizzie Andrew Borden
hold up your right hand.
Mr. Foreman,
look upon the prisoner.
Prisoner,
look upon the foreman.

Look upon the carnage
and the burning of the dress.

Look upon the missing hatchet
and the lack of blood
on her clothes and in her hair.

Look upon the dysfunctional family
and the improbable search for sinkers.

What say you Lizzie Borden?
What say you Mr. Foreman?
What say you?

Yet Another Word From Our Sponsor

Got a moth problem?
Fed up with pesky insects?
Try Professor Peeper's Prussic Acid.
Just a few drops in a sealed container
and those pests are history.
It's fast, it's clean and odorless,
and perfectly safe.
Professor Peeper's Prussic Acid
is great for cleaning furs,
even your favorite seal skin cape.
And try Professor Peeper's Prussic Acid Paste
perfect for removing stains on axes and hatchets.
Professor Peeper's Prussic Acid and Paste.
Get some today!

The Hill and After

...

That Song

That song,
that damnable song!
Ta Ra Ra Boom De-Ay, my ass!

And those chanting little girls
outside my window.
I know what they can do with their jump ropes!

And why can't they get the numbers right?
It was nineteen whacks and ten!
And how many times do I have to say this:
She was NOT my mother!

Maybe

Maybe if it had been August 12th,
instead of August 4th.

Maybe if father had not come home,
or Abby had really gone out.

Maybe if they had been more generous,
or the menu had been more varied.

Maybe if she hadn't had a hatchet.

Maybe if it had not been so hot,
or if it wasn't on a Thursday.

Maybe if Uncle Morse had not dropped in,
or Emma had not left.

Maybe if the windows had not needed cleaning,
or Maggie had not felt ill.

Maybe if she'd had more chocolate.

Then these little things wouldn't happen.

Billy Borden

He comes to us
deranged,
with wild, matted hair
and bad teeth,
smelling like Sasquatch,
and mumbling words of encouragement
to his trusty hatchet.

Ellen Egan says she saw him
loitering around the Borden place
on that fateful day,
wearing a raincoat
and smelling.

Billy, whose main job
was removing rotting animals
from farmers' fields,
claimed he was the unacknowledged
son of Andrew Borden
about to be cut out of the will.

Interesting, except there is no proof
of an illegitimate son,
and no will has ever been found.

Which only shows,
if you are going to make up a story
of a new suspect in the case . . .
you might as well make it a good one.

Lizzie Borden's Pew

Lizzie Borden sits in her pew
at the Congregational Church.
She sits silently,
barely moving, barely breathing.
Her pale eyes glow in the semi gloom.

Her fellow church goers
edge away from her spot.
It's too cold . . . it's too hot.
They are uncomfortable.
They are afraid someone will do something.

Somewhere in New England
Lizzie Borden's church pew
sits refinished in a foyer.
Lizzie sits there still from time to time.
Shunned by the other spirits,
she looks around for a friendly face . . .
and finds none.

Party Time At Maplecroft

Maplecroft is lit up like Halloween in Dublin.
Lizzie is throwing another gay party
for Nance O'Neil and her theater crowd.
Lizzie is spending her father's murder money.
Maplecroft is filled with the sound of an orchestra playing,
the sight of writhing bodies,
the smell of liquor and cheap perfume.
There is too much laughter in the air.
Emma does not approve.
"We should still be wearing black," she says,
and wallowing in shame and disapproval.
The sound of another door closing . . . . .
The sound of her footsteps echoing away . . . . . .

Rachael Ray Counsels Lizzie Borden

First, get a good set of knives.
And loosen up, Lizzie!
Laugh loud and often,
open mouthed with arms waving!
Animate yourself, Lizzie!
But above all remember . . .
extra virgin olive oil.

Extra virgin olive oil
and a good set of knives!

Lizzie The Larcenist

They call her "Lizzie the Larcenist."
A light-fingered lady
with her large purse
and voluminous skirts.
"Lizzie Borden took an axe"
takes on a whole other meaning.

She shops in Providence,
Boston, and New York,
picking up a few things for her friends.
Her father is no longer there
to pay for her indiscretions.

She seems shadowed
by a team of psychiatrists
who hold secret meetings at night,
analyzing her case.

"She was the victim of incest," one says.
"Robbing as she has been robbed."
"She is a lesbian," claims another.
As if lesbianism and kleptomania
are symptoms of the same situation.

None of their theories can be proven.
They stroke their long beards to points
as gas lights waiver overhead.
Much like their expert opinions.

Fall River, 1902

The boys in their short pants
are having their summer fun
filching watermelons,
and shoving chips off the ice wagon.
They swim in their favorite waterhole . . .
and devil Lizzie Borden.

They stand in front of the house
singing that terrible song
over and over and over again.
They throw snowballs and rocks and
rotten eggs and
ring her doorbell and run.

They are abusive and cruel . . .
and juvenile.
Much like the editor
of the Fall River Daily Globe
with his yearly rant at Lizzie Borden.

Lizbeth Of Maplecroft

She is Lizbeth of Maplecroft,
lady of leisure
living up on the hill.
She doesn't see strangers.
She answers no questions.

She can be seen in the yard
on summer afternoons
scattering seed for the birds,
broadcasting corn for gray squirrels
who peer around tree trunks to make sure,
then climb on her arms and shoulders
as if Disney himself is doing the animation.

Her friends these days are birds and squirrels.
She is Lizbeth of Maplecroft.

Wanted

Wanted: Coachman, lover,
someone who doesn't mind
a strong-willed woman.

Applicant must keep his mouth shut
when instructed to do so.

Money not an issue.

Semi-attractive woman
with eyes of steel gray.

Strong enough to keep you in line, buster!

Handy with an hatchet.

Loves to have squirrels crawling
all over her.

A bit of a petty thief
and a stay at home,
but you can't have everything.

Inquire at 7 French Street,
Fall River.

The Little Bird

Pity the little bird
that once strutted freely
in the neighbor's yard
just trying to earn
a little rooster living.

Is it crisply fried now
and served for Sunday dinner?

Was Lizzie invited?

Or is it in the country now
crowing its fool head off
and chasing young hens?

Either way it is no longer on French Street.
When Lizzie Borden wants you gone . . .
you're gone.

Emma In Hiding, 1913

The Post reporter's pencil
scratches furiously in his notebook,
like a cat on a new braided rug.
Miss Emma has never been interviewed before.

Guilty? No!
she says.
Lizzie didn't do it.
No weapon was ever found.

And Lizzie loves animals,
she says,
dogs and cats and squirrels.
How could she do such a thing?

I had to leave the house on French Street,
she says.
I could not approve of activities there,
but decline to give details.

Some night they will come for me,
she says,
making a tight little bow with her mouth,
as she hides in the shadow of her fan.

Maggie In Montana

She sits in the side yard
watching the dust cloud
kicked up by the approaching pickup.
Bridget Sullivan, grown old and
alone now with so many memories,
so many stories to tell.

The man in the truck
is a radio man.
One of the new breed
of newsmen
come to interview the Irish maid
of Lizzie Borden
of axe-murder fame.
The Borden sisters called her Maggie.

He eases arthritically
from behind the wheel
trailing a long cord
attached to who knows what
in the bed of the pickup.

The cord follows him across the yard
and he stands before her
under a clear blue Montana sky.
It is spring and the nesting wrens
chatter excitedly
in anticipation of what they might learn.

For a long moment they stand there.
Finally he utters a word or two
and hands her the microphone,
like a lover handing her a bright red rose.

Lizzie's Last Request

It is Lizzie's last request
To hear that old Scottish hymn,
To have the grave bricked,
To lie sacrificially
At the feet of her father.

As if in supplication
And atonement.

Emma

She sits alone in her little room
in New Hampshire.
Sitting in the shadows
her back to the door
like Mrs. Bates in Psycho,
as dry as a fallen leaf
in November.

Still in mourning attire,
she scans last week's newspaper.
Her sister has died.

Emma holds her mouth in a tight little knot.
She knows how little she knows,
how few questions she asked.
Perhaps it was better not to ask
and not to know.

Her sister is dead.
She would like to get up
and go downstairs and tell someone,
but she might fall
and break a hip.

Together Again

They lie in a tight little family group
at Oak Grove Cemetery.
Andrew and Abby and Emma and Lizbeth.
Surely the tensions have eased by now.

Andrew presides over periodic meetings
discussing his business dealings.
A small gold ring still clings to his bony finger.

Abby is planning another meal of cookies
and Johnnie cakes, mutton broth
and overripe bananas.

Emma doesn't say or do much of anything,

And Lizzie . . . Lizbeth, I mean,
that great American symbol of "breaking away,"
is still here, all mouth and ass
like a baby bird
who never really left the nest at all.

My Ain Countrie

Stand very still
near the fireplace
in Maplecroft.

Listen,
to the pure alto notes
of that old Scottish tune

Lizzie Borden is dead;
and Vida Turner,
soloist at the Congregational Church,
has been asked to sing Lizzie's favorite hymn,
as were her wishes.

No one is there,
the room is empty.

The voice is fainter now
than in 1927.
But she sings there still,
in that empty room . . .
where no one came.

Here They Are At Last

At last they come to us
after all these years
at Swansea
at the Luther Museum.
A treasure trove of family photographs.
Uncle Morse looking prosperous
and business like.
Sarah Borden, young and happy
and unaware of her early grave.
And Andrew looking less like
the Andrew we knew,
softer and more friendly.
And here is little Emma,
"pickley," even as a child,
in her criss cross dress.

And there is Lizzie
age eight or nine,
with her straw hat and feather,
wisps of hair hanging down.
Her eyes are tired,
her mouth strangely tight.
Some people see sadness
and some see innocence.
I see a scared little girl
who has already seen too much
to ever find happiness.
A girl who already knows
she prefers pets to people.
A frightened little girl
already fearful for her future.

Digging Lizzie

I dreamed
they dug up Lizzie Borden's bones
and found her buried
with a secret amulet
and a typed confession inside.

I dreamed
she was buried
with the hatchet in her hand,
her secret lover by her side,
its sex as yet undetermined.

I dreamed
they found the note to Abby,
and two porcelain plates with Tilden and Thurber
price tags still attached.

I dreamed
James Starrs stood by the grave,
a big smile on his face,
holding up a small sack of sinkers
for all to see.

Then I woke up
and found that,
if they did dig up Lizzie Borden,
they would find the remains
of a sixty-seven year old woman
who died of complications
from gall bladder surgery.

And nothing more.

Does Lizzie Go Back To The House At Night?

Does Lizzie go back to the house at night?
Does she stand in the room by the stairs?
Does she still see her father slumped on the couch?
Does his blood run red in her hair?

Does she sit in the heat in Maggie's room?
Is she out in the yard eating pears?
Does moonlight glint from her blade at night
In that room at the top of the stairs?

www.ingramcontent.com/pod-product-compliance
Lightning Source LLC
LaVergne TN
LVHW091312080426
835510LV00007B/476